ST PATRICK'S DAY

ST PATRICK'S DAY

KAREN FARRINGTON

&

NICK CONSTABLE

CHARTWELL
BOOKS, INC.

This edition published in 1998 by
CHARTWELL BOOKS, INC.
A division of BOOK SALES, INC
114 Northfield Avenue,
Edison, New Jersey 08837

Produced by
PRC Publishing Ltd,
Kiln House, 210 New Kings Road, London SW6 4NZ

ISBN 0 78580 950 3

Printed and bound in China

ACKNOWLEDGEMENTS
The photographs for this book were kindly supplied by the following:

Archive Photos: 94 (left)
Archive Photos (Kean): 14, 15, 34
Bord F·ilte/Irish Tourist Board: 7, 12-13, 17 (top), 22, 26, 27 (top), 36-37, 38, 39, 44-45, 46-47, 53, 60, 68, 69, 70-71, 73, 81, 83, 84, 92, 97,
98, 99, 100, 101 (top), 103, 104, 105 (top), 116, 117, 124 (left), 126, 130, 131, 132, 134
BPL: 54
Colour Day/Image Bank: 139
Steve Dunwell/Image Bank: 66, 106
Grant V Faint/Image Bank: 128-129
Alan Freed: 6, 96, 102, 105 (bottom)
The Hulton Getty Picture Collection: 10, 11, 16, 17 (bottom), 18-19, 21, 27 (bottom), 30, 40-41, 50-51, 55, 57, 58-59, 62, 76, 77, 78-79, 80,
107 (bottom), 113, 114, 115, 118, 119, 122, 124-125 (main picture), 135, 136, 137, 138
David Llyons: 3, 20, 23, 24-25, 28 (top and bottom), 29, 31, 32-33, 35, 42, 43, 48-49, 120-121
Maenza Photography: 52, 67, 85, 86, 87 (top and bottom), 88-89, 101 (bottom), 107 (top), 108-109, 110 (top and bottom), 111
Pictor International: 133
Andrea Pistolesi/Image Bank: 140-141
Reuters/Mark Cardwell/Archive Photos: 144
Reuters/Win McNamee/Archive Photos: 94-95 (main picture)
Reuters/Peter Morgan/Archive Photos: 64-65
Reuters/Mike Segar/Archive Photos: 91
Reuters/John Stillwell/Archive Photos: 123
Marc Romanelli/Image Bank: 143
Jeffrey M Spielman/Stockphotos, Inc/Image Bank: 127
Carol and David Thalimer: 4, 61, 72, 74 (top and bottom), 75 (top and bottom), 82, 93
Earl Young/Image Bank: 112

CONTENTS

INTRODUCTION

ABOVE: *An Irish piper in traditional garb rallies marchers during the 1996 Pittsburgh parade.*

OPPOSITE: *Two girls begin a pilgrimage to the peak of Croagh Patrick, Co. Mayo, in 1976. The mountain, where Patrick is said to have fasted, is one of Ireland's holiest places.*

A FEW YEARS AGO, Irish men and women regarded St. Patrick's Day as a somber occasion, a time to spend with the family, attend church, and reflect on the life's work of their greatest and most enigmatic preacher. Right up to the 1970s pubs in Ireland were shut by law on March 17 and the festival was celebrated with Gaelic sports meetings, the odd ceilidh, a fireside story, and, for a few hardy souls, a pilgrimage to the summit of Croagh Patrick in Co. Mayo.

So what happened? How did a religious festival celebrating the arrival of a captured slave fifteen centuries ago, reinvent itself as today's all-singing, all-dancing global party in which half the English-speaking world seems to claim Irish ancestry? What drives Americans to dye rivers and ski slopes green, march in their thousands behind pipe bands, sell green beer and green bagels, paint their faces (yes, green) and spend wads of dollars on shamrocks—a plant which graces just about every meadow in Ireland?

It is the same in Australia—where some seven million people claim Irish lineage—New Zealand, Canada, and much of Europe. Even the sheikhs of Abu Dhabi raise a green champagne cocktail on Patrick's feast day and in Moscow—where once only macho military parades would do—the Novy Arbat throngs with families cheering on bands of shivering majorettes. Wherever you are in the world, it is somehow easy to be Irish for the day.

Cynics say that it is all down to the machinations of big business. Certainly the likes of Guinness have done well out of the St. Patrick's Day phenomenon, and even the burger bar giants McDonald's (who can hardly claim to serve traditional Irish fare) have cashed in. As one of their most painful advertising jingles, broadcast in the 1970s, used to say: "Hey, come on down. The weather's getting better. Have a big thick shamrock shake. We'll welcome in the spring together."

In fairness, Americans at least have a long-standing tradition of running St. Patrick's Day hooleys. The worldwide parades we see today originated in the U.S., partly as a means of military recruitment during the Revolutionary and Civil Wars and partly as a cultural statement for the waves of Irish immigrants who arrived in the eighteenth and nineteenth centuries. These settlers, strangers in a strange land, sought to celebrate their roots in the way they knew best—with marching, music, feasting, and storytelling.

This is not to suggest that their new life offered plenty and security; far from it. The first settlers, in the eighteenth century, were Scots-Irish, tough frontiersmen whose family roots lay in the war-torn border country between England and Scotland.

These fiercely proud non-conformist Protestants established townships in Pennsylvania and Maryland, expanding their lands tortuously into the Wild West. Hundreds died at the hands of (equally proud) Native Americans, living conditions were harsh and comforts few. It was a long and bloody road.

The second major influx of Irish settlers came in the mid-1800s. They were mainly Catholic farmers; refugees from the great potato famine, undernourished, emotionally scarred, and pitifully poor. They settled first in East Coast cities such as Boston and New York, worked for a pittance as casual builders and laborers, and were immediately treated as an underclass. Too often, job

RIGHT: *Homeward Bound! During the nineteenth and early twentieth century, passenger liners did a roaring trade between America's East Coast ports and the British Isles. Judging by his outfit, this emigrant could easily afford his fare home.*

BELOW: *The Kennedy family has perhaps the most influential voice in Irish-American politics. Tragically, an assassin cut down President John F. Kennedy in his prime.*

PREVIOUS PAGE: *The statue of St. Patrick, serene in Slane Friary at sunset. The Hill of Slane is the supposed site of Patrick's challenge to the Druids.*

ABOVE: *The nine counties of Northern Ireland as portrayed in a map drawn c. 1914. They have rarely been free from the trauma of civil war.*

RIGHT: *The thirty-two counties of Ireland. This map dates from the early eighteenth century.*

A GENERAL MAPP OF IRELAND

advertisements carried the sinister footnote: "No Irish Need Apply."

For both of these groups, St. Patrick's Day offered an opportunity to boost morale, to honor the mother-country, and, most importantly, to prove that they would not be downtrodden. Street parades, marching bands, clubs, and societies helped establish a tradition which was later adopted by Irish communities around the world. It was these spirited pioneers who shaped the St. Patrick's Day festival that we know today.

This book aims to chart the known history of the saint, his influence on the Irish people and culture, and the growth in popularity of his feast day. It cannot claim to be a definitive account of his life (much of which has, in any case, been turned into myth by the early priests); nor does it give detailed accounts of his teachings. Instead, the intention is to show the faith, determination and bravery of one man who has inspired a nation at home and abroad. The Irish love and respect him. They are right to be proud of his legacy.

RIGHT: *Monks marching through Dublin in 1996 aim to remind the Irish that St. Patrick's Day is a time for Christians to reflect; not just an excuse to get drunk.*

ST. PATRICK FACT AND FICTION

St. Patrick—Who Was He?

ABOVE: *This drawing, commissioned many centuries after the saint's death, offers a typical portrayal of him preaching to the masses. Patrick's long beard and aged features reinforces the idea that he, like Moses, was blessed with longevity.*

RIGHT: *Patrick the Bishop. The serpent beneath his right foot is supposed to symbolize his defeat of paganism.*

HISTORIANS have always struggled with St. Patrick. Considering that he shaped the face of Ireland, persuading proud and ferocious warriors to abandon their natural gods for Christianity, precious little has emerged about his life. Beware the Irish expert who claims to know the "real" Patrick. In the fifth century A.D., history was largely recorded in the form of story-telling—embellished as necessary—rather than the written word. This aside, it is beyond question that St. Patrick was a courageous and hugely successful missionary.

The arguments about his life start with his birthplace. This has been variously ascribed to Cornwall, Cumberland, Kilpatrick (near Dumbarton, Scotland) the mouth of the River Severn, and Boulogne, on the French coast. In a sense, the geography is unimportant. The British Isles, and much of western Europe, was peopled by similar Celtic tribes, also known as Ancient Britons. Indeed, an increasing body of academic opinion suggests that the "Celtic" civilization, as such, was merely a myth and that culture in many parts of Europe evolved simultaneously along similar lines. Certainly, our modern conception of political boundaries means little. There were, for instance, numerous "Irish" settlements in Devon, Cornwall, and Scotland.

Even Patrick's name is subject to dispute. The names Magonus, Succetus, and Patricius are all attributed to him—he appears to have settled on the latter once his work in Ireland began. However, his identity was further confused after his death as "rival" Patricks emerged from the mythological miasma that characterized the Dark Ages. This culminated in an unseemly war of words between the Irish bishops and the monks of Glastonbury, England, who claimed that he was buried at their monastery. The political machinations of early Christian leaders do not, thankfully, belong in this book.

So what can we say of Patrick? He was born between A.D. 387 and 415, probably in Wales or the west of England, and raised in a nobleman's family. His father was a church deacon and local government official, although

ABOVE: *Prehistoric stone circles such as this are relatively common in Ireland. Many have links to Druidism and "earth magic" and would have been considered citadels of evil by the early Christians.*

ABOVE RIGHT: *The stone-carved Cross of St. Patrick and St. Columba in Co. Meath.*

BELOW RIGHT: *The crowded harbor at Boulogne in north-west France. The town has a strong claim to be the birthplace of Patrick, although historians have also mounted cases for the West of England, Wales, and even Scotland.*

there was little sign of a devout upbringing. Patrick later admitted he was "careless" about religion, and his father, Calpurnius, seems to have been more interested in the tax advantages associated with a church position. The family's estate would have been an obvious target for the Irish raiders then pillaging Britain's western seaboard. At age sixteen, Patrick was captured by the Celtic king Nial Navigiallach, (Nial of the Nine Hostages) and taken back to Ireland as a slave. He was subsequently bought by the pagan chief Miliac, of Slemish Mountain, Co. Antrim (the precise location is disputed) and put to work as a sheep herder. As we learn from the two Latin works attributed to Patrick—*Confession* and *Epistle To Coroticus*—it was those six, lonely years on a hillside that forged his faith in God. He tells how one night he heard a voice cry out, "Thou fastest well, and soon shalt return to thy country." Later the same voice added: "Behold, a ship is ready for thee."

Patrick fled his post and journeyed some 200 miles to an unidentified Irish port where he saw a ship waiting. At first he was refused passage but, while he prayed for guidance, a member of the crew found him and shouted, "Come along, they are asking for thee. Come, we will take thee on trust." The captain, it seems, had agreed to let the youth pay his fare later. In fact, Patrick did settle this debt by producing a herd of swine for the starving crew after they arrived at their destination in Northern France. (See *Patrick's Miracles.*)

From this point on, the chronology of events becomes confused. Patrick seems to have returned to his family for a while before experiencing a dream in which a man named Victoricius (probably a bishop of Rouen) presented him with a letter headed, "The Voice Of The Irish." Patrick tells how he heard "the voices of those who dwelt beside the wood of Foclut which is nigh to the western sea, and thus they cried, as if with one mouth: 'We beseech thee, holy youth, to come and walk among us once more'."

He traveled to Auxerre and there began his formal education as a priest under the direction of the famous French bishop Germain, or Germanus. Some years later, around A.D. 431, Pope Celestine ordered another bishop, Palladius, to begin the conversion of Ireland—a mission which began well. However, within a year pagan leaders grew suspicious of Rome's motives and felt that their power base was threatened. Palladius hastily returned to the safer shores of Britain, and died soon afterwards.

It now fell to the newly consecrated Bishop Patrick to take over the Irish mission, an event enshrined in the old adage: "Not to Palladius, but to Patrick did God grant the conversion of Ireland." He landed near Wicklow sometime between A.D. 432 and 460 but was repulsed by the local tribe. Undeterred, he set sail again, this time arriving at Lecale in Co. Down. Here Patrick encountered the pagan chief Dichu with a band of armed warriors but managed to convince him that there was no cause for alarm. Within days, Dichu had become his first convert.

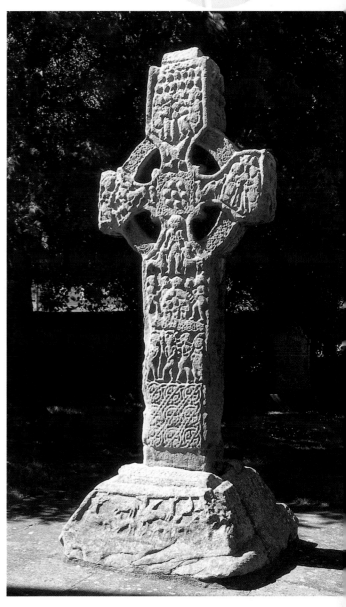

RIGHT: *The Severn Bore—a wave which ripples for miles up the River Severn at Bristol in western England. According to one legend, Patrick was captured from a well-to-do Romano-British family living in this area.*

ABOVE: *The chiseled features of St. Patrick's statue at Slane Friary, Hill of Slane, Co. Meath. Near this site Patrick is said to have challenged the might of the druid priests by daring to light a fire in defiance of the spring festival of Beltane.*

It is spontaneous conversions such as this which cynics find so hard to accept. After all, Dichu's entire life and culture had been built around pagan magic and natural gods. Why throw it all away on the basis of one stranger's enthusiasm for an unknown, crucified, preacher? Christians would cite this as an example of the power of God. Many historians would argue that Ireland was not quite so isolated from Christian teaching as was once supposed.

It seems likely that, by the time Patrick arrived in Ireland, there was already a healthy scattering of Christians in the 200,000-strong population. The new religion was imported by captured French and British slaves and, as the Roman empire broke up, so Irish pillagers brought in more outsiders. Coupled with a flourishing sea trade between Ireland and Europe, it is easy to see how Christianity could have spread without the need for direct church intervention. Dichu would surely have heard of Christ, even if he was not a baptized believer.

Second, Patrick would have been preaching to an audience desperate for protection in an uncertain political climate. To many, the known western world seemed on the verge of collapse, and apocalyptic prophecies about the Day of Judgement would have been widespread. The atmosphere can be likened to that of Europe in the first half of the twentieth century, when established order seemed under constant threat and rival powers competed for supremacy. Against a similar background, Christianity would have offered shelter from the gathering storm.

Third, Patrick arrived as an established bishop, rather than a missionary in the usual sense. The conversion of Ireland was not an experiment conducted by Rome; rather, it was a chance to apply lessons hard-learned throughout Europe during earlier centuries. Patrick was a highly-trained operative whose duty was to minister to an existing community as much as rove among the heathen. This is not to say that he avoided danger; on the contrary, his life must have been threatened often. "Daily I expect murder, fraud or captivity," he wrote. "But I fear none of these things because of the promises of heaven. I have cast

BELOW: *Glastonbury Abbey as it looks today. Bizarrely, the monks of Glastonbury claimed for centuries that the body of St. Patrick was buried with them. Only in later years did Christian historians manage to sort out the mass of confusion which surrounded a number of Irish holy men named Patrick.*

"Across the sea will come Adze-head
crazed in the head,
his cloak with hole for the head,
his stick bent in the head.
He will chant impiety
from a table in the front of his house
all his people will answer:
'Be it thus. Be it thus'."

Another version of this poem reads:

"Adze heads will come over a furious sea,
Their robes hole-headed,
Their staves crook-headed.
Their altars in the east of the houses
All will answer: 'Ame'."

myself into the hands of God Almighty who rules everywhere."

At least he would have had disciples and a crude organization on which to found his mission. He took a practical view of missionary work; often arriving before a suspicious warlord with presents of money and finery. Once he had secured an audience, his training as a preacher took over.

It was this training, and mastery of debate, which so easily outflanked the resident druid magicians. They took refuge in vague cults and established tradition. Patrick had heard it all before from his slave-boy days. He would have been sensitive to pagan Irish practice and probably adapted traditional beliefs where they were compatible with Christian doctrine.

There was one other crucial advantage that he had over the pagans. Their own arch-druids had long predicted his arrival. (See box at left.)

The political geography of fifth century Ireland must have been a major obstacle to the mission. There was no clear pecking-order of rulers; indeed, there was no concept of nationhood at all. Occasionally, some warlord or other would declare himself a *Triath*, a High King said to rule "through the kingdoms of Ireland from sea to sea." If this ever really happened it was so rare and so brief as to be of little consequence.

The idea of a one-nation medieval Ireland was encouraged by later scholars determined to prove that all the great families and rulers were united by descent from a single colony of ancestors. The *Book of the Taking of Ireland* espoused this theory, which historians today regard as completely discredited. It may have suited warring kings to wrap their constant bickering in some semblance of unity but it bore no relation to historical fact.

The reality was that Ireland represented a genetic melting pot for native Irish, Briton, Celt, Roman, and Gaul. For the best part of a thousand years, it was a place locked in civil war between pagan tribes. Battles against the Vikings and Normans would come later; though even then the Irish fought against each other to settle old scores and improve tribal power bases.

In Patrick's day, rulers tended to fall into three distinct groups: the petty kings or *Ri Tuaithe* (those with small estates), the *Ruiri* (supposed overlords of several *Ri Tuaithe*), and the *Ri Ruirech*, kings of a particular province. The petty kings controled things at local level, their fiefdoms expanding or contracting depending on bargains struck and treaties made.

LEFT: *The beautiful coastline at Greystones, Co. Wicklow. St. Patrick is reputed to have landed near here sometime between A.D. 432 and A.D. 460. He was repelled by local tribesmen but later docked at Lecale in Co. Down.*

BELOW: *A detail from the east face of the Cross of St. Patrick and St. Columba, Co. Meath. The figures on the left are Adam and Eve; on the right, Cain is in the act of murdering Abel.*

Later, power would concentrate among the great family dynasties of the provinces—the Ui Neills (Ulster), the Ui Dunlaigne (Leinster), the Ui Fiachrach and the Ui Briuin (Connaught), and the Eoganacht (Munster.) For Patrick, each family dynasty and sub-dynasty had to be won in turn. Christian principles such as forgiveness must have been difficult to fathom for warriors raised on blood feuds.

Perhaps one of the saint's greatest legacies was the way that he brought together rulers and religion; imposing a sense of order in barbaric times. Royal patronage was vital to the monasteries because it ensured protection. However, kings were rebuked if they oppressed the masses or sought undue influence. When the Ulaid tribe attacked one of Armagh's churches in A.D. 809 (long after Patrick's death) its leaders suffered terrible retribution. The powerful King Aed Oirnide invaded Ulaid territory and put the ringleaders to the sword.

RIGHT: *The tiny memorial church at Saul, known as Sabhul in the fifth century A.D. It was here that he founded his first Christian community and he returned to it often as a spiritual retreat. He is thought to have died at Saul while fighting illness under the care of St. Brigid the healer.*

ABOVE: *The statue of St. Patrick with his holy mountain, Croagh Patrick, rising in the background.*

ABOVE RIGHT: *A version of St. Brigid's Cross. The design is still widely used in Irish brooches and jewelry.*

BELOW RIGHT: *The tomb known as St. Patrick's Grave at Down Cathedral. Patrick's death and his final burial place are not well documented: this is one of the locations that . claims his grave.*

Following the conversion of Dichu, Patrick resolved to seek out his old master, Miliac, and win him for the cross. This was easier said than done. According to legend, Miliac heard that Bishop Patrick was coming, gathered together all his worldly goods and set fire to his house—vowing to die with honor rather than bow to his slave's religion. Smoke was still curling above the ruins when Patrick arrived. "Why," he cried to his followers, "would this king consign himself to the flames to avoid believing at the end of his life? Only God knows."

Patrick set up his bishopric or "see" among the Ulaid in what is today known as Ulster. Armagh has long claimed to be his Irish home and the two great cathedrals bearing his name—one Roman Catholic, the other Church of Ireland—today face each other across the city from two hills. However, Patrick also had strong links with the west and conducted much of his missionary work there. We know that he journeyed across the plain of Connaught, built churches in Sligo and Roscommon, and once ascended Croagh Patrick, Co. Mayo, to spend Lent.

Around A.D. 443 he left the north and Meath in the hands of Bishop Secundinus, while he and his followers explored Leinster and Munster. Seven years later he left the region, after preaching from a hill to hundreds of his followers. From this point on he seems to have divided his time between Armagh, supervising construction of a cathedral, and Sabhul (also called Saul), his favorite spiritual retreat and the spot where he built his first church.

It was here, soon after completing his *Confession*, that Patrick was stricken by a terrible illness. He was under the care of the healer Brigid, later St. Brigid, but she was unable to save him. In his final days he apparently tried to

return to Armagh but ·was turned back to Saul by an angel. He died on his feast day, March 17 (also his birthday according to legend), some time between A.D. 465 and 493.

News of the saint's death spread rapidly across Ireland and the clergy responded with a huge celebration of his funeral. Contemporary writers talk of extraordinary pomp and a festival of light which was so intense that at night "even darkness was dispelled." According to the ancient hymn of "Fiech," the sun refused to set.

FAR RIGHT: *Holywell beneath the stone fort Grianan of Aileach in Co. Donegal. It was here that St. Patrick is supposed to have performed his first christening on Irish soil.*

RIGHT: *The stunning cliff scenery at Malin Head, Ireland's most northerly point. St. Patrick's experiences at sea must have made him acutely aware of this treacherous coast.*

BELOW: *Beehive-style monastic huts. These are the remains of an early Christian settlement on the summit of Skellig Michael, an island off the coast of Co. Kerry*

Although he had given Ireland a common Christian faith, Patrick could do little about the tribal feuds which so often dogged his work. After his funeral a dispute broke out over where the body should be interred and, to avoid bloodshed, all sides eventually agreed on a site in Co. Down. This was reportedly rediscovered in 1185 and the remains transported to another, undisclosed, location.

Today, 1,500 years on, what is the legacy of Patrick's life? The strictly historical view is that he was a great preacher, an educated man, and one of the most successful missionaries ever. Even so, stories of his awesome power and miracles must be taken in context. Many of these were conjured up by priests in much later times to keep the laity true to their faith. Almost any flamboyant story was acceptable provided it saved souls.

Today, Patrick remains Ireland's greatest, and most mysterious, folk hero. The songs about him are ludicrously banal; reliable portraits are in short supply, and there is not a single great work of sculpture to commemorate his life.

Perhaps he would have wanted it like this. He came to Ireland not as some reluctant colonial servant of the church (the lot of Palladius) but as a priest who genuinely loved the country and the people who once enslaved him. Today, he exists in the minds of the Irish worldwide as a national apostle and a guiding spiritual light. What saint could ask more?

FAR RIGHT: *A grotesque stone head found at an early monastic community near Lower Lough Erne, Teampull Mór, Devenish, Co. Fermanagh.*

RIGHT: *St. Patrick's Cross at the Rock of Cashel, a fourth century fortification once the capital of the old kingdom of Munster. Conversion of important pagan settlements would have been a top priority for Patrick's mission.*

PATRICK'S MIRACLES

THIS IS WHERE HISTORICAL FACT AND FICTION start to blur. Patrick rarely mentioned miracles. In fact, his writings tend to portray a genuinely humble man acutely aware of his own ordinariness. In Butler's *Lives Of The Saints* there is reference to him being guilty of a sin while still a boy of sixteen. "He committed a fault which appears not to have been a great crime, yet was to him a subject of tears during the rest of his life."

The problem facing the clergy after Patrick's death was that the Irish church needed a figurehead to demonstrate the might of God. Irish pagans had been raised believing in natural magic and the power of the druid shape-changers. Unless the church could show that it had greater power, there was a risk that newly-won converts might start reverting to the old ways.

So monks and priests did a public relations job on Patrick. Hagiographies were compiled extolling his powers, miracles appeared in vague anecdotes, and folk stories warned of terrible vengeance wreaked upon those who dared challenge the saint and his God (see *Patrick's Flame*). The clergy seemed to have few scruples about making these things up. This was a well-oiled propaganda campaign, justified by the saving of souls. The more miracles invented, the greater the saint.

Many of these were modeled on druidical legend. Patrick turned his followers into deer in order to protect them from enemies. He was able to pass through locked doors. He could transform day into night. These or stories of similar feats had once been used to support the hierarchy of pagan priests. Now, it seemed, Patrick could both match and exceed their powers.

One miracle is acknowledged in his *Confession* and occurred while he was still a young man, shortly after he escaped from

slavery. His ship landed in Brittany, France, and Patrick found himself wandering with the pagan crew through a land battle-scarred by pillaging Frank warriors. They had hoped to sell their wares but found no custom and no food.

After a month of this the travelers, close to death from starvation, began to plead with their captain to lead them to safety. He turned to Patrick and said, "Christian! Thy God is powerful. Pray for us for we are starving." The saint asked them to kneel with him and, after a few moments, a herd of swine came crashing through the undergrowth. The crew chased and killed many of them and halted for two days to recover their strength. Later, they found some wild honey and presented a portion to Patrick as an offering of thanks to God.

Patrick also refers to a rather curious vision or dream that occurred immediately after eating the roast pork. He tells of his fear as Satan appears and tries to roll a massive boulder onto his chest. Patrick screams out, "Elias, Elias." He writes, "Thereupon the splendor of the sun shone on me and dispelled all the burden on me." Some scholars say this is evidence of him invoking a saint or holy man, presumably the prophet Elias, but it is more likely the use of the Roman word for sun, "Helios." This would explain his reference to the sun shining.

It does seem incongruous that a Christian preacher should be seeking help from what is, after all, the focus of pagan worship. But at the time Patrick had received no formal tutoring in theology, and his beliefs were probably a mish-mash of half-Christian, half-heathen, thinking. Also, "Helios" had passed into the language as an exclamation, something akin to "oh, my God" today. In writing of this experience in his *Confession*, the saint gives no clear indication of what he really meant.

ABOVE: *Sun worship was an integral part of pagan doctrine and Patrick's period of slavery among the heathen Irish would have familiarized him with their beliefs. According to one account of his trials with Satan, he calls for help by crying "Helios, Helios" (the Roman word for Sun). This suggests something of the tangled thought processes that perhaps existed for many years—even among Christian preachers.*

PATRICK'S FIRE

ABOVE: *St. Patrick leading followers into battle against King Leogaire and the druid priests at Tara. On the way they sang the hymn now known as "St. Patrick's Breastplate."*

THIS IS ONE OF the best-known stories about St. Patrick. It neatly sums up the determination of the Irish church to confront and defeat pagan ways—hence the direct power struggle between Patrick and the druid magicians. But there is a more subtle message in that the saint's arguments for Christianity are seen to overwhelm those of the druids. The point of the tale is simple. Not only is God more powerful; his way makes more sense.

In fifth-century Ireland it was the druids' custom to celebrate the spring festival of Beltane (the return of the sun's power) with a fire ritual. This involved extinguishing fires across the land for several days; then lighting a single bonfire at the Temple of Temora, on top of the deeply sacred Hill of Tara. Hundreds of people would gather for the ceremony, among them the greatest noblemen and the most powerful magicians.

Patrick may well have chosen to confront the pagans at Tara because of its ancient royal and spiritual history. Or he may just have been staying close by. Either way, he resolved to celebrate Easter near Tara and led a band of his followers across the plain of Bry to the Hill of Slane. As they walked they sang the hymn which became known as "St. Patrick's Breastplate," or "The Lorica."

On his arrival at Slane, Patrick pitched his tent and at nightfall kindled a fire. The flames were spotted by King Leogaire and his assembled nobleman at Tara, and created instant panic. Their own Beltane fire had not yet been lit; the festival had not begun. Who was responsible for this sacrilege?

The king summoned his druid priests, who warned that, unless this strange fire was quickly extinguished, it would overpower their flame and bring his kingdom to a swift downfall. Leogaire assembled warriors, guests, and his two most senior priests in 27 chariots, and rode to within a short distance of the saint's tent. There he ordered the company to seat themselves and to refuse to rise when the Christian rebel was brought in front of them.

Leogaire's warriors hauled Patrick before their king. All remained seated save one small boy called Herc, son of Drogo, who rose to his feet. (Patrick blessed him and later made him Bishop of Slane.) The saint was ordered to declare his aim in coming to Ireland and contend the following day with the Magi (druid wise men) on the subject of religion. It may have been at this point that Patrick stooped to pick a shamrock and use it to explain the three-in-one doctrine of Catholic theology—the Father, Son, and Holy Ghost.

The story of this Easter Day battle was clearly intended to mirror Moses' tussle with the Egyptian magicians and, perhaps, also Elijah's victory over the prophets of Baal. Much of it seems to be pure fiction, the work of later clergy, and several events described are quite absurd.

In one account Leogaire's chief druid, Lochru, rises into the air to prove the power of his religion. As he screams abuse at the Christian faith, Patrick is overcome with righteous anger and shouts: "O Lord who can do all things, who sent me here. May this wicked man who blasphemes Your name be carried out of here and die straightaway."

An unseen angel then throws a giant snowball at Lochru from the heavens which flips him into the air and smashes him down, shattering his skull on a sharp stone. At this Patrick cries "May God arise and his enemies be scattered." Pandemonium ensues. Darkness falls on the camp, the ground shakes, Leogaire's guards attack each other and horses stampede. The terrified king kneels before Patrick, though in his heart he remains an unbeliever.

ABOVE: *The view across St. Patrick in Slane Friary, Hill of Slane, Co. Meath. The high ground of Tara is just visible in the top center, at the left of the picture. It was from here that Leogaire recoiled in horror at the sight of Patrick's Fire.*

Later, Patrick and his followers march boldly into the king's castle and burst into his banqueting hall. There follows a final contest with the remaining druid, Luctmael, which ends in the magician's fiery death, and Patrick tells Leogaire, "Unless you believe now, you will soon die, for God's wrath will come down upon your head."

Whether this threat worked or not is debatable. It seems Dubtach, an eminent Druid bard, did submit to the faith and dedicated all his future poems to Christ. According to more reliable accounts, the king was not converted but agreed to let Patrick freely preach the word of God. The victory at Tara, however it came, gave the saint a kudos and mystique which became a powerful weapon against his pagan enemies.

RIGHT: *The Boyne valley at Slane. According to legend it was somewhere near here that St. Patrick picked a shamrock to help teach the principles of Christian faith.*

PATRICK
AND THE SNAKE

ABOVE: *The Lough Derg pilgrimage center in Co. Donegal. Spiritual retreat seems to have been a key part of Patrick's teachings.*

DRAWINGS OR PAINTINGS OF ST. PATRICK very often show him crushing or killing a snake. These may be based on folklore that claims he drove all the snakes out of Ireland (there were actually never any there in the first place) but is more likely to be an acknowledgement of his primacy over the old religion, the pagan earth-magic of the druids.

The snake traditionally represented paganism in early theology. When Patrick is depicted with power over snakes he is, metaphorically, driving out the old ways and replacing them with Christ's message.

Another idea is that the snake was closely associated with fertility and the essentially female character of Irish paganism. Goddess-worship was commonplace, and for hundreds of years priestesses held positions of great power within Bronze and early Iron Age communities. Some historians believe that the

"snake" of feminine superiority in Ireland needed to be fully subjugated by the new masculine Godhead.

An example of this is the story of Patrick and the monstrous serpent of Lough Derg (where pilgrims today flock to pray at St. Patrick's Purgatory). Medieval texts record that he banished the monster by striking it with the "golden rod of Jesus," given to him by an elderly hermit in Gaul. Folklorists are more subtle, claiming the saint persuaded it to stay at the bottom of the lake until "La Luain" (which it understands as Monday). However, "La Luain," in old Irish, also means Day Of Judgement or Last Day. Consequently, the monster is confined for ever.

Yet another theory on Patrick's iconography is that he is not crushing the snake but is supported by it. Pragmatic early Christians often tried to connect with pagan beliefs rather than

ABOVE: *Penitential beds—an uncomfortable resting place for Christians seeking atonement at Lough Derg.*

stamp them out by force. (There is over-whelming evidence for this throughout the British Isles, where early churches are often sited at or near pagan sites.) The supporting snake, linked to fertility and healing, is thus absorbed into Patrick's mission.

RIGHT: *St. Patrick's Purgatory at Lough Derg, one of Ireland's most important pilgrimage sites. It was here that the saint is said to have banished a huge serpent. Some say it was through the power of a golden rod; others believe Patrick simply outwitted the monster.*

PATRICK AND THE SHAMROCK

According to a traditional Irish rhyme:

"There's a dear little plant that grows in our isle 'Twas St. Patrick himself, sure, that set it; And the sun of his labor with pleasure did smile And with dew from his eye often wet it."

ABOVE RIGHT: *The weather-worn surface of Carndonagh Cross, regarded as Ireland's earliest Celtic High Cross, at Carndonagh, Donegal.*

RIGHT: *The "unfinished" cross which stands in the churchyard at Kells, Co. Meath.*

THE SHAMROCK MAY NOT BE Ireland's official emblem (that honor falls to the harp), but it holds the same meaning for the Irish as does the rose, thistle, and leek for the other nations within the British Isles.

Legend has it that St. Patrick used the shamrock as a way of explaining the Holy Trinity—God the Father, Son, and Holy Ghost—to the pagan Irish. The impression often given is that this was a totally alien concept to heathen Celts; in fact, the reverse is true. The Irish were probably receptive to the Trinity because it resembled their own triadic pagan philosophy. As a canny and pragmatic preacher, the opportunity to exploit this similarity would surely not have been lost on Patrick.

Another old verse, with religious undertones, reads:

"This plant that blooms forever
With the Rose combined,
And the Thistle twined,
Defy the strength of foes to sever.
Firm be the triple league they form
Despite all change of weather;
In sunshine, darkness, calm or storm."

RIGHT: *The Rock of Cashel, Co. Tipperary, was the ancient fortress of the Eóganacht family dynasty. Its founding ancestor, Oengus, is said to have been blessed and baptized by Patrick.*

THE THREE PATRICKS

T HIS RANKS AMONG THE MOST PUZZLING episodes in the whole St. Patrick phenomenon and illustrates the intense rivalry and political infighting endemic in the church at the time. The historical ramifications rumbled on for centuries, generally muddying the waters for scholars studying the saint's life. Readers who find historical characters and chronology confusing should prepare for the worst.

Apart from the original and genuine Patrick, two other saints of the same name, medieval period, priestly rank, and geographical area were recorded by contemporary writers. The first was a bishop Patrick of Avernia or Auvergne. He seems to have been the result of a basic blunder by a cleric who copied down Avernia instead of Hivernia (the Roman-period name for Ireland and Scotland) thus causing a duplication. No such saint existed in Auvergne, but to be on the safe side he was given a feast day anyway—March 16.

There was also a Patrick Senior, whose life is commemorated on August 4. According to the medieval writings of Ranulph of Chester, this Patrick was an Irish bishop who retired to Glastonbury in the year A.D. 850 and died soon afterwards.

Had this man been the real Patrick, it would have meant the saint had a 350-year lifespan.

You might have thought that such an obvious impossibility would have ruled out any confusion. Not so. For one thing, some priests did refer to the real Patrick in his last days as "Sen Patrick" or "Senex Patrick" (literal translation: "the old man Patrick"). Also, writers of martyrologies such as *Lives Of The Saints* were determined to bestow upon St. Patrick a lifespan equal to that of Moses (so emphasizing his holiness).

The result of all this was that the archbishops of Armagh found themselves with rival Patricks in their records. Irish writers tried to resolve the debate by making clear that the Patrick Senior buried in Glastonbury could not possibly be the real saint, because of the timespan involved. (The thought of Ireland's spiritual mentor being buried in England was, in any case, too much to bear.) However, the Glastonbury monks were having none of that. As far as they were concerned they had the remains of the right St. Patrick, and it was he that they knew as "Sen Patrick."

ABOVE: *The Cooley Peninsula and nearby Carlingford, Co. Louth, have been important Celtic settlements for thousands of years.*

PATRICK's CONFESSION

AND HIS

EPISTLE TO COROTICUS

THESE TWO DOCUMENTS, written in fifth century Latin and in similar style, are generally accepted as the only surviving writings of the saint. *Confession* isn't actually a confession at all as we understand the word today. Instead, it is a semi-autobiographical self-defense against accusations brought against him by (presumably envious) senior clerics in Britain. It is from this that we learn of his early life and his duties as a slave. He also explains why he felt it necessary to leave his bishopric for a while to deal with a direct personal command from God. The financial matters he mentions were probably connected with funding this mission.

The tone of the writing suggests Patrick knew he was close to death. He speaks of Ireland as a largely Christian country with ordained clergy in every province. He gives thanks to God for assisting him and leaves instructions as to how the work

should be continued. He also expresses hope that the world, and especially his family back in Britain (who had so opposed his Irish venture), should know how God had prospered through his work. He says it is for this reason that the book is written in Latin, his native tongue, rather than the Erse language of the Irish. Self-effacing to the last, he apologizes for the crude style and blames this on his infrequent use of Latin over the years

The *Epistle* was addressed to a warlord active in Western Britain at the time. Coroticus had seized several young Irish Christians, all followers of Patrick, and herded them off as slaves. This was an act mirrored in Patrick's own past, which is perhaps why he felt so strongly about it. The writing is full of moral outrage and denunciation.

ABOVE: *The impressive Dun Eochla stone fort on Inishmore, Aran Islands, Co. Galway. Isolated pagan settlements such as these became the focus of Patrick's mission to Ireland.*

UNPREDICTABLE
PATRICK

This story concerns Patrick's search for a site on which to build his cathedral, at Armagh. According to the *Book of Armagh*, the saint had set his heart on a particular hill and asked the owner, a man called Daeri, if he could use it. Daeri refused and offered him a plot in the valley instead.

Perhaps feeling guilty, Daeri then visited Patrick and presented him with a large cauldron, finely wrought and imported from overseas. "Gratias again" (I thank thee), said the saint. Daeri went home muttering: "What a fool that fellow is to say only Gratzacham for a wonderful cauldron containing three firkins. Ho! slaves, go and fetch it back to me again."

So the slaves went and brought back the vessel. "Well," said Daeri, "what said he to you churls?"

They replied: "He said Gratzacham again."

Daeri considered for a moment. "Gratzacham when I give and Gratzacham when I take away. The saying is so good that for these Gratzachams he shall have his cauldron back again. Ho! slaves, take the vessel back to Patrick." Daeri accompanied them on the errand and to show his good nature gave the saint the hill he wanted.

ABOVE: *A view of "Patrick Country." The slopes of Croagh Patrick tower above the rippling surface of Lough Derg.*

TAKING THE CELEBRATIONS WITH THEM

ABOVE: *One of the imaginative floats at Chicago's St. Patrick's Day parade.*

RIGHT: *Shamrock City. A scene from Dublin's 1996 parade.*

CURIOUSLY, IRELAND cannot claim any credit for inventing the St. Patrick's Day parade. The idea emerged in the United States at the end of the eighteenth century, first to assist military recruitment of the Irish during the War of Independence; later as a celebration of Celtic heritage.

The concept was copied by Irish ex-pats around the world and has gradually expanded to include the wild shenanigans we see today. When you drink your green Guinness, tuck into your green mashed potato, and wave your inflatable shillelagh at the local theme-pub's version of a ceilidh, you are participating in the export of a national culture. These days it may be commercially driven but its value in raising Ireland's profile on the world stage is inestimable.

To understand the global growth of St. Patrick's Day it is important to establish why millions of Irish men and women emigrated in the first place. This is a huge and complex issue but there are some generally accepted historical markers which help set the scene.

There had been a trickle of emigration from Ireland to the British mainland and the Low Countries of Europe for decades up until the turn of the eighteenth century. However, the ravages of civil war and five failed harvests caused by bad weather, meant that by the early 1700s the trickle had become a flood. The prospect of a new life in the fertile lands of North America was too much for many to resist.

These initial émigrés were mainly "Scots-Irish"—nonconformist protestants whose ancestral roots lay in the war-ravaged border country between England and Scotland before their resettlement in northern Ireland. They were a fierce and proud people, who endured horrendous conditions in the first migrant ships. Most settled in Pennsylvania and Maryland and established townships on the frontiers of the Wild West.

It was a hazardous life. Estimates suggest that for every Native American killed, 50 Irish settlers were either kidnapped or killed by Indian tribes. Despite this daily threat, it is thought that around one quarter of Ireland's 2.3 million population left for the colonies during the seventeenth and early eighteenth century.

They arrived at a time of colossal change and upheaval. Resentment at Britain's authoritarian rule was being voiced publicly and settlers were angry at the prospect of punitive taxes on imports—"taxation without representation" many called it. Frustration boiled over at the Boston Tea Party (1773), during which a group of radicals (including some of Irish stock) dumped a cargo of tea into the harbor in protest at

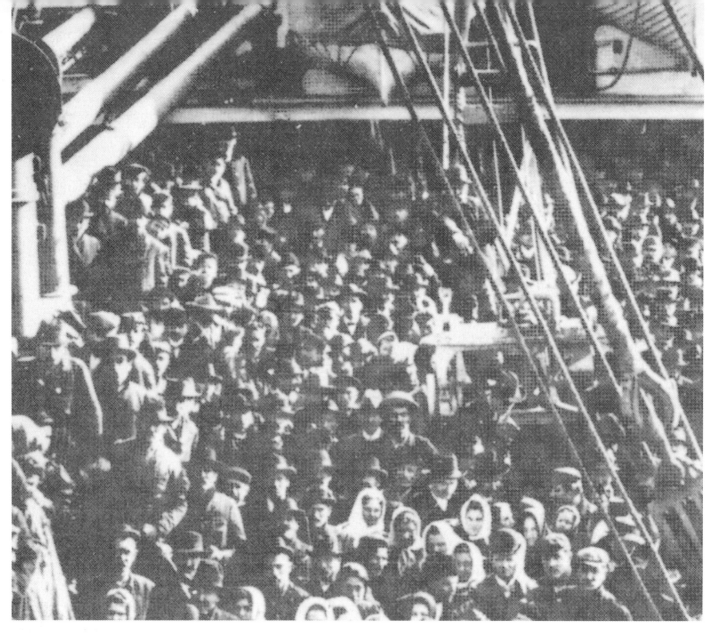

ABOVE: *Hundreds of Irish emigrants prepare to set foot on American soil for the first time. Between 1841 and 1925 more than five million made the arduous voyage across the Atlantic.*

RIGHT: *An artist's impression of the Boston Tea Party; a defining moment in American history. This drawing shows radicals tipping tea into the harbor in protest at the British government's policy of dumping cheap tea onto the U.S. market. Two years later the American War of Independence began.*

Britain's policy of unloading cheap tea onto the American market. London responded with the drastic "Intolerable Acts" and within two years the American War of Independence had begun.

The war brought hard choices for Irish-Americans, both catholic and protestant. True, their whole reason for emigrating had been the poor quality of life back home, but some recognized that this was as much down to difficult economic factors (and poor harvests) as it was to the indifference of the government. Besides, not all the Irish had been welcomed with open arms on arrival in their new land. The poorest were regarded as slave labor and treated accordingly. Against that background the call of their king (Ireland was, of course, part of Britain) remained a powerful draw.

The British army recruiters were well aware of this and used St. Patrick's Day parades as a chance to remind the Irish of their homeland and their duty to fight for the king (the increasingly insane George III). Not to be outdone, the rebel colonists staged their own recruitment parades—emphasizing the status of migrants as independent Irish-Americans. Not for the first time, St. Patrick found himself at the center of a propaganda war in which each side tried to out-Irish the other.

Although Scots-Irish settlements were barely two genertions

old, their culture had already taken root. St. Patrick's Day became a focus both of worship and celebration and Irish ballads were the popular music of the day in areas such as Charleston, Carolina and along the Shenandoah Valley. The influence of these songs is undiminished even today. Much of the Country and Western music emerging from Nashville is indistinguishable from traditional Irish songs. "The Clog Step" for instance—used in Nashville's square dances—is a direct descendant of the good, old-fashioned Irish jig.

The War of Independence was drifting towards stalemate (the Americans winning the north; the British largely controlling the south) when the royal commander, Cornwallis, made the mistake of ordering his troops directly into the interior of the southern colonies, the Scots-Irish heartland.

Unfortunately for the British these tough frontiersmen had won their lands in a bloody guerilla war against the Indians. The British army held little fear for them. When Cornwallis finally surrendered to French and American forces at Yorktown, Virginia, in 1781, American independence was assured. It was acknowledged by London two years later in the Treaty of Paris.

For the Scots-Irish pioneers, nationhood heralded a new dawn. Instinctively restless, they moved on to Arkansas and from New Orleans up the Mississippi River. There they met third generation Scots-Irish coming down the Ohio from Pennsylvania and the colonization of the west continued apace through the likes of legendary figures such as Davy Crocket (the son of a Londonderry immigrant.)

The legacy of the St. Patrick's Day parade was to give the Irish settlers a clear symbol of their roots. The first, held in New York City in 1762, was followed by parades in Philadelphia (1780) and Savannah, Georgia (1813). Quickly the event became known as the "Wearin' of the Green," a call to take pride in all things Irish.

The Savannah event is particularly interesting. For one thing it was assiduously recorded by the organizers; for another, it began a tradition of inventiveness that continued right up to the 1960s with an attempt to dye the Savannah River green (more of which later.)

The city's procession was conceived by the oldest Irish organization in America, the "Hibernian Society," formed by thirteen protestants in 1812. The following year they gathered for a private parade to the Independent Presbyterian Church and in 1818 a military Irish unit—the "Fencibles"—arranged a similar march. On March 17, 1824, Savannah's first public St. Patrick's Day parade got underway.

These early gatherings retained a strong military emphasis. In Savannah the Irish "Jasper Greens" regiment provided an armed escort and fired a salute at the end to signal the dismissal of all marchers. According to the records Irish clubs and societies were: ". . . all dressed in their respective regalia and bearing their beautiful banners."

Most of the groups would assemble before the parade for an annual general meeting to elect officers and discuss financial

matters. This meant that afterwards they could get down to the serious business of drinking and merrymaking. As the "Hibernian Society" secretary of 1845 put it: ". . . (marchers) partook of a meal at the City Hotel. Songs and sentiment ruled the festive meeting until the adjournment of members to their respective homes."

The 1870 procession was the first in Savannah to adopt an overall chairman—the "Grand Marshal of the St. Patrick's Day Parade." Five years later the first recorded floats took part, with one wagon carrying women representatives of Ireland and America; another contained thirty-two women dressed to resemble the thirty-two counties.

The year 1875 also saw the largest-ever participation of Irish catholics and an early indication that the "Wearin' of the Green" had strong commercial potential for Savannah's retailers. It was noted that, "the clothing stores that year, even as today, displayed green neck ties and gloves and shamrocks placed in the buttonholes of coats and in the bands on all of their hats."

Occasionally the city was forced to postpone its festival (though torrential rain in 1853 "did not dampen the spirit" of the local Irish). In 1862 and 1864 the Civil War made it impossible to organize; in 1913 the date coincided with Holy Week; in 1918 it was hit by the turmoil of World War I; and in 1921 as it was halted in a gesture of solidarity with the Irish Revolution.

Whereas most of the early settlers were protestant, the mid-nineteenth century saw the arrival of Irish catholics in large numbers. Their migration began as the result of social factors; namely that Irish farms—the staple of the

RIGHT: *The Treaty Oak at Austin, Texas, is thought to be over 500 years old. Comanche and Tejas indians held tribal rites beneath it and it was supposedly the venue for the first boundary treaty between European settlers and Native Americans. Not all encounters between old and new cultures were so civilized—as the Scots-Irish discovered.*

RIGHT: *This exhibit of potatoes helps remind visitors to the Famine Museum at Strokestown Park House, Co. Roscommon of the two million Irish people who died during the great blight of 1845-51.*

RIGHT: *Marchers prepare for one of the truly great Irish-American celebrations — the St. Patrick's Day parade at Savannah, Georgia. In 1961 organizers thought up the idea of dying the Savannah River green as an eye-catching centerpiece. The plan only partly succeeded but the idea was successfully borrowed by Chicago.*

country's economy—had become smaller with each generation. Farmers divided and subdivided their land to allow their sons independence and the chance to raise a family. Soon the farms were not big enough to provide a living.

The Irish Potato Famine of 1845–51 proved the final straw. This devastating crop blight was a disaster unparalleled in Europe since the days of the Great Plague and at least a million died of starvation. Faced with the prospect of no home-grown food, no alternative work, and mass evictions, it is little wonder that families abandoned everything and boarded the famine ships for America. The causes, and the British handling of the crisis, are a constant source of debate—especially among revisionist historians with political axes to grind. However, the one inarguable truth is that the Irish, particularly the catholic poor, suffered appalling privation, while their political masters in London delivered a hopelessly inadequate response.

The scale of emigration was breathtaking. Before the famine the population of Ireland had more than doubled to 8.5 million. By 1851, it was down to 6.5 million. In 1847 alone, 250,000 left

ABOVE: *Irish families waiting for a ferry to take them to one of the large (and always overcrowded) emigrant ships. In most cases their initial destination would be the slum areas around New York, Boston, and Philadelphia,*

for America and Australia with thousands more migrating to Britain. Between 1841 and 1925 more than five million Irish arrived in the U.S., 70,000 went to Canada, and nearly 400,000 to Australia. News of the mid-nineteenth century gold rushes, centered on San Francisco and Melbourne, fueled wild rumors of lands dripping in gold and silver.

The exodus of women (especially to the U.S.) was particularly apparent. By the mid-nineteenth century Ireland's agricultural economy had moved from crop-based farms to livestock production and the number of jobs available was drastically reduced. Irish parents still expected their daughters to do farm or shop work but for little or no wages. They also stopped subdividing their farms, preferring to hang on to grazing land, so that family estates were passed on through wills. This in turn meant that sons inherited land much later in life — and consequently married later.

Irish women had to compete for husbands by offering a good dowry of land, cash, or cattle. Those whose families could not afford this were left to a spinster's life and by 1920 a staggering one in four Irish women aged 45 to 54 had never married. No wonder so many looked across the Atlantic for work, often tagging along with relatives.

In the nineteenth and early twentieth centuries Ireland was the only country to send as many women as men to America and, for a few decades, Irish female immigration actually exceeded that of males. The emerging U.S. middle classes needed single women as domestic servants and Irish house-maids found that they were in hot demand. A woman could make between 50 and 75 cents a week (plus tips and lavish presents if she was lucky,) and be guaranteed bed and board on top. Many acquired reputations as "good savers." Unlike their male counterparts there was little they needed to spend.

It would be wrong to imagine though that the Irish settled quickly into lives of domestic bliss "below stairs." Unlike the (mostly wealthy) German, French, and Dutch farmers who migrated, the Irish were invariably poor and unable to purchase property. They fitted quickly into the role of second-class citizens—digging quarries, laboring on building sites, suffering hunger and cold during the lean winter months. There are heart-rending stories of young Irish men lying about their status for fear of losing face. Letters home might boast loudly of a new career at the bank; in reality it would be as a floor sweeper.

New York, Chicago, Philadelphia, and particularly Boston, where many famine ships disembarked, became the key Irish catholic centers. Home would be a waterfront shanty or over-crowded tenement, diseases such as tuberculosis were rife, and the infant mortality rate was higher than any other social group. There is evidence to suggest that the average life expectancy of Irish settlers was as low as six years.

With unemployment high, literacy low (school was an expensive luxury), and a temptation to turn to drink, the Irish became victims of racism.

A prejudice emerged in which the Irish were cast as drunken slum-dwellers, whose grandmothers smoked clay pipes, and whose families survived on the slaughter of a backyard goat or pig. Ironically, organizations such as the "Ancient Order of Hibernians"—often criticized today for promoting "shamrock sentimentalism"—were formed precisely to rid Irish-Americans of their stereotype.

St. Patrick's Day dances, marches, and feasts were not just about showing solidarity or shedding work-a-day pressures. They were a symbol that the migrants belonged and that they occupied a respectable strata of society. Moreover, the hundreds who turned out for St. Patrick's Day parades helped challenge America's image of the Irish as alcoholic ruffians. Not only could these men stand up; they could actually walk in time.

Inevitably, the parades were a focus for resentment as well as celebration. In Toronto, Canada, the city fathers regarded the Irish as loose cannons—an unpredictable element in a community proud of its Anglo-Saxon sense of order. St. Patrick's Day parades tended to be the spark for sectarian tensions between protestant and catholic.

When the Fenian (Irish republican) leader, Jeremiah O'Donovan Rossa, arrived to deliver a lecture on March 18, 1878, he encountered a feverish atmosphere. His speech on Irish liberty resulted in a major riot which brought chaos to downtown Toronto. Gunfire was exchanged, rocks hurled, and there was widespread looting of shops. Rossa was forced to go into hiding. Soon afterwards the city ordered a ban on St. Patrick's Day parades, an order which lasted until 1988.

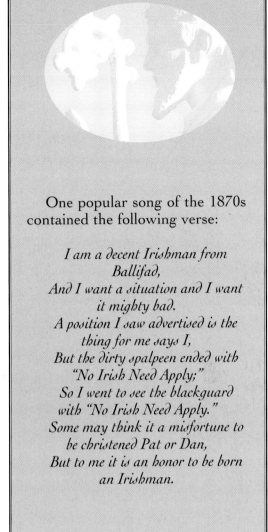

One popular song of the 1870s contained the following verse:

I am a decent Irishman from Ballifad,
And I want a situation and I want it mighty bad.
A position I saw advertised is the thing for me says I,
But the dirty spalpeen ended with "No Irish Need Apply;"
So I went to see the blackguard with "No Irish Need Apply."
Some may think it a misfortune to be christened Pat or Dan,
But to me it is an honor to be born an Irishman.

RIGHT: *A marching band prepares to move along Fifth Avenue during the 1996 St. Patrick's Day Parade in New York. The city hosts the largest parade in the world and attracts more than a million spectators. Its roots lie in the need to portray the Irish as respectable citizens.*

BELOW: *Boston's 170 year-old Quincy Market. The city of Boston hosts one of America's biggest St. Patrick's Day parades.*

ABOVE RIGHT: *Shamrock power in the Chicago parade.*

BELOW RIGHT: *The Chicago skyline. The city has a population of some 240,000 Irish-Americans.*

In Australia the need to celebrate Irish heritage was perhaps even more important. The American Revolutionary War had forced the British government to find a new destination for the expulsion of its convicts and the colonies of Australia and New Zealand were obvious choices.

The first transportation ship to sail directly from Ireland was the *Queen*, which arrived in Port Jackson on September 26, 1791. Over the ensuing sixty-two years, some 30,000 Irishmen and 9,000 women were sent as felons to serve a minimum period of seven years. Some of these were political rebels, others had committed acts of theft out of desperation during the famine years. Despite this background—and the fact that many Irish migrants were soldiers who had faithfully served Britain in the Napoleonic Wars—there remained a stigma about Irish-Australians which had to be addressed.

The emergence of St. Patrick's Day celebrations in North America was a trend enthusiastically copied. As well as the

ABOVE: *A medieval theme at the 1996 Dublin Parade.*

RIGHT: *Dublin marchers get into the festival spirit. Mingling in the crowds are the Green Detectives who hand out instant prizes to anyone who has opted to "Dress Loud; Dress Green."*

OVERLEAF: *Spectators dressed for the occasion enjoy the parade.*

parades, some communities organised Gaelic sports events, harp recitals, Irish suppers and ceilidhs. But to many families the feast day remained intrinsically linked to the church and was a time for family gatherings and sober reflection about the old country.

The Irish "invasion" occasionally took the authorities by surprise. On April 9, 1850, Melbourne's first catholic bishop, James Goold, laid the foundation stone of a new church in what had once been a sheep enclosure. Building work began, but within two years the explosion in Melbourne's Irish population forced a rethink. Bishop Goold decided the church would be too small to cope, pulled down the partly-completed structure and built a bigger one in bluestone. In 1858 he went still further, commissioning the great English architect, William Wilkinson Wardell, to design a cathedral incorporating part of the unfinished church. Today, St. Patrick's Cathedral, Melbourne, ranks among Australia's finest buildings.

LONGEST RUNNING

ST. PATRICK'S DAY PARADES

New York	1762
Philadelphia	1780
Savannah	1813
Montreal	1824
Carbondale, Penn.	1833
Chicago	1843
New Haven, Conn.	1845
San Francisco	1852
Scranton, Penn	1853
Atlanta	1858
Cleveland, Ohio	1867

LEFT: *A solitary young patriot held up by his hat at the Dublin festivities in 1997.*

BELOW: *Traditional travel at the Savannah celebrations in 1992.*

FAR LEFT: *Savannah's colorful floats attract thousands of visitors and provide a major boost for the local economy.*

ABOVE: *Savannah's children are made well aware of their Irish heritage—both at school and at home.*

RIGHT: *A traditional meeting point for Savannah marchers.*

LEFT: *An impressive image of St. Patrick in Bishop's garb at the Savannah celebrations. According to legend, the shamrock in his left hand was used to explain the Holy Trinity to the pagan Irish*

BELOW: *Packed streets in Savannah.*

THE ST. PATRICK'S BATTALION

ABOVE: *American army general Zachary Taylor seen directing his troops at the Battle of Buena Vista, Northern Mexico, during the Mexican-American war. Many of Taylor's Irish soldiers deserted to the Mexican cause, sick of being ill-treated by their officers. Sadly, they fared little better on the other side.*

THE STORY OF THE ST. PATRICK'S BATTALION is one of bravery, despair, and inhumanity. It illustrates all too clearly how Irish settlers in America were thrust into a war that meant little to them, how they were abused by their own officers, and how they paid the ultimate price in mass executions.

In May 1846 the United States Army, under Brigadier-General Zachary Taylor, was camped on the northern bank of the Rio Grande River. The U.S.–Mexican war had just begun—due to a culmination of a dispute over national boundaries—and Taylor was preparing to invade Mexico from the recently-annexed state of Texas.

Among his troops were many Irish catholic migrants, new arrivals who had encountered a wave of hostility from more established white settlers. Anti-Irish gatherings—even riots—were seen in Boston, New York, and Philadelphia and catholics bore the brunt of rejection and discrimination. With no other prospect of work, it is little wonder that they sought refuge in the army. The St. Patrick's Day military recruitment parades, with their stirring music and colorful banners, evoked a new spirit of adventure and hope. The reality, of course, was very different.

The conditions endured by Taylor's army were appalling. Men huddled in cold, leaky tents, diseases such as dysentery were widespread, and food was barely edible. Officers meted out harsh punishment at the slightest provocation, and dispirited men were bound, gagged, and flogged by indifferent superiors. Neither was the army an escape from anti-Irish sentiments.

The Mexican generals were well aware of this and mounted an effective propaganda campaign, playing on Irish patriotism, to encourage mass desertion. Turncoats were promised Mexican citizenship and 320 acres of land (more for officers,) if they swapped sides. At least 260 of Taylor's recruits, mostly Irish, accepted the offer.

Conditions in the Mexican Army proved even worse. But it was too late to go back. The Irish deserters found themselves fighting former comrades in the battle of Monterrey (won by the United States) and then marched 300 miles south to regroup. In December 1846, at San Luis Potosi, the St. Patrick's Battalion was officially formed with Brevet Major Francisco Rosendo Moreno in command. Moreno's second in command was Lieutenant John Riley, an Irishman with a reputation for bravery, if not loyalty. He had joined the United States Army two years after deserting the British in Canada.

Throughout the winter of 1846/47 the St. Patrick's, or St. Patricios as the Mexicans called them, became part of a cat and mouse game which the advancing Americans could not fail to win. With generals such as Robert Lee and "Stonewall" Jackson directing military strategy, and reinforcements of 10,000 additional troops, it was only a matter of time before Mexico City fell.

Despite these odds, the St. Patrick's Battalion bought Mexico some breathing space. The Irish soldiers defended a crucial bridge at Churubusco with such ferocity that they repulsed six United States' regiments over five hours, the

BELOW: *Native Americans prepare a fire to cook the day's meal. Warriors like these proved brave, skilful, and ruthless opponents for Irish settlers seeking to establish themselves in the Wild West. Some estimates suggest that, for every Native American killed, 50 Irish settlers were either killed or kidnapped by tribes.*

stiffest resistance of the entire campaign. They fought beneath their banner—the figure of St. Patrick, the Irish harp, and the shamrock on a green field—and apparently took grim satisfaction in shooting their former bully-boy officers.

One reason for their defiance was knowledge of the certain fate facing deserters. Three times their Mexican comrades tried to run up the white flag of surrender and three times the Irish pulled it down, killing one flag holder in the process. When the bridge was taken, the battalion retreated to the nearby convent of Churubusco to make a last stand. They gave in only when the Americans' heavy artillery rolled across the bridge and began to pound the convent.

The seventy-one surviving St. Patricios faced court-martial on August 28. Four pleaded guilty, the rest claimed they had been captured and forced into the Mexican Army while in drunken stupors. Riley escaped hanging because he had deserted before war with Mexico was declared. He and twenty others were each given fifty lashes of a bullwhip and branded with the letter D on their cheeks.

Of the remaining fifty, two were shot and sixteen were hanged quickly. The other thirty were forced to stand for two hours on an elevated gallows at Mixcoac, nooses around their necks, to watch the American army storm Chapultepec Castle. They were told they would be executed when the Stars and Stripes was raised above the castle, Mexico City's last stronghold.

When the dread moment came that day—September 13, 1847—it is said that the Irish gave one last, defiant cheer. Today, a plaque in their memory, close to the church of San Jacinto in San Angel, reads: "In memory of the soldiers of the heroic St. Patrick's Battalion, martyrs who gave their lives for Mexico during the unjust American invasion of 1847."

RIGHT: *Frontier country c. 1800. Scots-Irish settlers needed huge mental resilience to survive the battles with Native Americans.*

THE "REBEL" SHAMROCK

RIGHT: *The General Post Office in O'Connell Street. During the Easter Rising in 1916 it was taken over by the Irish Volunteers and the Irish Citizen Army as part of a plan to control Dublin's communications.*

BELOW: *Irish National Volunteers saluting the flag at Keash, Co. Sligo.*

REFERENCES TO WEARING A SHAMROCK on coat lapels, in honor of St. Patrick's Day, first surfaced in Britain in 1681. During Grattan's Parliament, in the late eighteenth century, it became an emblem for troops of the "Irish Volunteers," but by the reign of Queen Victoria it was regarded as a symbol of rebellion and Irish regiments were forbidden to display it. Irish civilians showed their contempt for this by wearing a paper cross colored red and green.

CELEBRATIONS TODAY

ABOVE: *Another scene from the parade at Savannah. Georgia. In 1961 local resident Tom Woolley grabbed world headlines with his plan to dye the river green in honor of St. Patrick.*

THESE DAYS YOU DON'T actually need to be Irish to have a hooley on St. Patrick's Day—although in America, Canada, and Australia it is difficult to find someone who, on March 17, *doesn't* claim ancestry from the "auld sod." Most of Europe tends to be baffled by the fuss but goes along for the ride anyway. Muscovites parade along the Novy Arbat, Germans attempt "Danny Boy" in Frankfurt's "Irish Zone" pubs, Parisians focus on high-Celtic culture, Belgian bartenders pump out ceilidh ditties at disco-volume, and the Brits simply embrace a new reason to party. Even the oil sheikhs of Abu Dhabi raise a glass—traditionally champagne and green creme-de-menthe.

The St. Patrick phenomenon may be spreading apace, but it is in the U.S., where the modern celebrations began, that it has assumed truly mind-boggling proportions. If there's a way to flaunt your Irishness you can bet your granny's gilded shamrock that the Americans have found it, colored it green, and given it the full begorrah. That is why green Guinness is now almost as famous as the black stuff; why you can buy green bagels on the streets of New York City; why the Niagara River at Buffalo is dyed green (makes a change from toxic orange according to the local wags) and why, in the "Irish Alps" of Massachusetts you can find yourself skiing on green snow.

It wasn't always like this. Irish-Americans used to be content with a good parade, a tot of whiskey, a plate of bacon and cabbage, and a rousing chorus of *The Star Of The County Down*. Somewhere along the line, St. Patrick's Day got bigger and decidedly extravagant. The city of Savannah, Georgia, probably takes the credit, or blame, depending on your point of view.

Savannah is an outstandingly beautiful old city. Founded by the English settler James Oglethorpe in 1733, it is laid out in 22 squares, each with a central park containing huge magnolia trees and giant oaks covered with moss. The Irish flocked here in their hundreds during the eighteenth and nineteenth cen-

BELOW: *River-dyeing comes to Ireland as workmen prepare to turn the River Liffey emerald green in honor of St. Patrick.*

turies and today around 14,000 residents claim Irish ancestry—around 10 percent of the population.

For years Savannah's St. Patrick's Day festivities tended to be a family affair, largely unnoticed by the rest of the world. Then at the beginning of March, 1961, Tom Woolley, thirty-six-year-old food director of the city's DeSoto Hotel, made a chance remark to an Irish-American colleague about making everything more up-front. As Woolley later told the *Savannah Morning News*: "No one knows the heritage of the Irish in Savannah. They always think of New York and Boston. You have a big day, but nobody knows about it but you guys."

Woolley idly mentioned a plan to dye the Savannah River green. Within days the idea had leaked out and fired public imagination. A local chemical company offered to donate hundreds of gallons of dye, thirty private boat owners agreed to dump it in the water, and even the U.S. Navy got in on the act—providing a helicopter to fan the dye into an even mixture. At four o'clock on the afternoon of March 17, a siren sounded and a flotilla of small craft, lined up across the river at Habersham Street, chugged away.

Sadly, their efforts were in vain. The water was so choppy that boat skippers decided to turn back three blocks early at Whitaker, rather than cruise up to Montgomery Street. The 3,000 spectators who had braved the wind and cold were expecting to see brilliant green water; what they got was merely greenish. Gradually, Savannah's Irish headed for more traditional celebrations in the nearest bar.

One resident, Jimmy Coleman, who was eight at the time, recalls: "Everyone walked away. It was like, 'So what. Where's the green beer?' The river just looked darker. It did have a green tinge to it but the river's so nasty anyway. It just looked a little more nasty."

Morning News reporter Archie Whitfield said: "Everybody thought the entire river was going to turn a magnificent, solid green and sit that way for a couple of days and everybody could go down there and see how pretty the river is."

He remembers arriving at Mayor Malcolm Maclean's office in the City Hall to get some official reaction. "I walked in and said: 'Your Honor, what do you think about the river? Did it turn green?' And he said something to the effect of: 'I officially proclaim the Savannah River green.' But I have an idea he was thinking: 'What a mess, what a joke, What are these Irishmen going to try next?'" Mayor Maclean was more positive. "I thought it was a good idea," he said. "They were just trying to make it a bigger day. It gave everybody a lot of laughs."

Woolley insists the event was no failure. "The river did go green," he said. "With a little more sunlight and a little less silt it would have been even greener. I have pictures of it (taken from the air.) You could see the river's all green. Well, it was striped green at that point, like a zebra."

Woolley was named honorary St. Patrick's Day Mayor and later became a guest on the popular U.S. television game show *I've Got A Secret*. He moved to Charlotte, North Carolina, the

ABOVE: *Dyeing the Chicago River. Tough anti-pollution laws have reduced the amount of dye released and ensured there is no danger to fish.*

ABOVE: *Mayor Daley prepares to lead Chicago's parade in 1962. Politicans know that active participation in St. Patrick Day festivities is essential to secure the Irish vote.*

following year and never attempted the dyeing stunt again. The idea was taken up by Chicago's Mayor and continues today with the greening of the Chicago River

Savannah, though, got its day of fame and branded itself on the American psyche as an important Irish center, rivaling New York, Boston, and Chicago. The knock-on effect for hotels, restaurants, bars, and souvenir shops helped stoke the local economy and in the days before tourism became a year-round industry it meant the difference between financial buoyancy and bankruptcy. Traders relied on the spending power of 400,000 St. Patrick's Day partygoers to see them through the quiet times.

Inevitably, Savannah's parade got a national reputation for inspiring the unexpected. The year after the green river fiasco a group of young women paraded topless along River Street, resulting in a new twist to the Gaelic greeting *Erin Go Bragh*. It was, said onlookers, more a case of "Erin Go Bare." Police were less amused, arresting several women and video-taped the rest ("to provide evidence in court," they said).

Not everyone in the city regards St. Patrick's Day as a

LEFT: *Dyeing the Chicago River at speed. City fathers insist the idea was not copied from Savannah but emerged when pollution control officers used colored dyes to trace illegal discharges.*

BELOW AND NEXT PAGE: *Pushing the boat out in Chicago. St. Patrick's Day is a lucrative business for the scores of pleasure boat operators.*

drinking binge (drinking in, or during, the parade is now banned by the organizers). Many old Irish families still follow the traditions of private banquets, their houses decked in green ribbons and streamers. Above all, it is a time when grown-up children, working away, make every effort to go home. To them, the feast day is quite as important as Christmas or Thanksgiving.

Enthusiasm for St. Patrick does tend to flow in and out of fashion. In Chicago, for instance, the parade tradition dates back to 1843 when 770 people turned onto the streets. It was suspended in 1896 and over the next sixty years became something of a forgotten anachronism. Then a new generation of Irish-Americans began to seek their cultural roots and the parade returned, with a new, glitzy image. This included the crowning of a "Queen of the Green" (the first was Florence Babusek Gallagher) and the greening of the river.

Chicago, naturally, insists that its river-dyeing tradition is not some blatant copy of Savannah's original. According to city historians it began in 1962 when teams working on pollution control started using colored dyes to trace the source of illegal discharges. One city plumber apparently emerged with green-colored overalls and this inspired Stephen Bailey, a union leader and close friend of the then Mayor Daley, to come up with a Savannah-style ceremony, only better.

That year a hefty 100 pounds of powerful, vegetable dye were slowly released—enough to keep the river green for a week. These days, the aims are more modest. Forty pounds of dye is enough to provide two or three hours' worth of green water.

As America's ethnic base has increased, so too has the diversity of cultural events. Boston in 1950 could boast an Irish population of almost 70 percent, and the story goes that, when downtown trains passed St. Ambrose Church, half the passengers instinctively crossed themselves. Now the Irish are as likely to be found in neat, middle-class suburbs as they are in their traditional inner-city strongholds. They currently comprise

around twenty-two percent of Boston's community. In contrast, the number of Hispanic incomers has increased 64 percent between 1980 and 1990.

When representative James Brett failed in his attempt to run for Mayor in 1993, he partly attributed the result to this dilution of the Irish vote. "Mrs O'Malley and her seven children—all registered to vote in Dorchester's Ward 13—are no longer there," he ruefully concluded.

Watching a St. Patrick's Day Parade in, say, Holyoke, Massachusetts, illustrates the social change clearly. The Irish are still there, of course. But now the route is also lined by Poles, Russians, Haitian, Hispanic, Moldovan, Cambodian, Vietnamese, and African immigrants all sporting "Kiss Me—I'm Irish" hats and licking emerald-green candy floss. No one is suggesting they are resented—racism has never been an Irish trait—but the unique spirit of many parades has gone forever.

Boston has adapted to this by turning what was once a simple, day-long street party into a full-blown Irish festival lasting a month. It helps that March 17 is a local holiday (Evacuation Day—the commemoration of George Washington's expulsion of British warships) and that the city has a long tradition of putting St. Patrick first. In the past this even required special dispensation from Boston's bishops to skip the demands of lent; no Irish family was going to miss out on its traditional corned beef, cabbage, and potato supper.

New York, which boasts the world's oldest civilian parade, has a special role to play. In 1998 N.B.C. broadcast live T.V. coverage of this event for three-and-a-half hours—an indication of its importance to Irish America. Visitors to the city are confronted by a Tricolor on every main street, by green ice-cream, green mashed potatoes, green bagels and (inevitably) green beer. Bar owners say that it is the only date on which their staff cannot take a day off.

You can buy special little lapel pouches in which a shamrock is fixed in its own mini-vase (to keep it fresh) and St. Patrick's Day greeting cards which play *When Irish Eyes Are Smiling* (courtesy of microchip technology.) Even the Empire State Building gets bathed in green light as the main procession draws to a close in the evening.

Parade themes have become both fashionable and political. San Francisco called its 1998 gathering "Peace In Northern Ireland For The Children's Sake," while Washington's assumed the grandiose title "Irish-American Youth—the Future of the Nation." Washington, particularly, has developed an acutely political flavor to its celebrations with several ceremonies emphasizing America's links with the "old countries."

The Washington parade is held on the Sunday before St. Patrick's Day, beginning in Constitution Avenue at noon and finishing in front of a specially-erected grandstand near the White House. The "Grand Marshal" is usually a prominent Irish-American politician or celebrity (the comedian Hal Roach received the honor in 1998) and he or she rides in a horse-drawn coach for the three-hour duration.

Like many U.S. cities, Washington revived its annual parade

ABOVE: *Dublin's classical architecture festooned with brightly colored bunting adds a shade of frivolity to the city's 1997 St. Patrick's Day festivities.*

comparatively recently. In the early 1970s marchers walked from Dupont Circle to Robert Emmet's statue in Massachusetts Avenue, close to the Irish embassy. However, this arrangement became fraught with difficulties after protracted street violence erupted in Northern Ireland. The authorities decided that the route skirted too close to the British embassy and ordered a rethink to avoid any unseemly diplomatic incidents. Diplomacy and high-powered political lunching have remained the order of the day. On the morning of March 17, the Irish ambassador (sometimes the *Taoiseach* himself) arrives at the White House for the traditional presentation of a bowl of shamrock to the President. This is followed by the Speaker's lunch on Capitol Hill, an event started by former Speaker Tip O'Neill in honor of the Northern Ireland Social Democratic and Labour Party leader and peace negotiator, John Hume. These days even the British embassy seeks to court the visiting Irish with a lunch hosted by the ambassador for visiting politicians and the media.

In Canada, Toronto has rapidly become the focus of Patrickmania. Considering the city's revived parade has been running only since 1988, the slick organization and general gusto of the festival truly illustrates the renaissance of Irish culture in North America. Toronto now proclaims March "Irish Month" and flies the Irish flag in front of the City Hall. There are a string of high-profile social gatherings, including the "Ireland Fund Luncheon" (a fundraiser for "peace and culture" in Eire) and the "Grand Marshall's Ball."

For those who take their drinking more seriously, there are dozens of Irish pubs offering a good laugh. These include the deliciously-named "Fionn MacCool's," "Scruffy Murphy's," "Quigley's," "Kitty O'Shea's," and the "James Joyce." The weekend before St. Patrick's Day sees many of these bars taking the equivalent of a quiet month's income within twenty-four hours. However, it is in Australia that the pubs have latched onto St. Patrick's Day, dusted it down and turned it into one long celebration of alcoholic excess. There are three main reasons for this. Firstly, the faux-Irish pub is now in just about

BELOW: *Enjoying the midday sun: Pittsburghers wait quietly for the parade to reach them.*

RIGHT: *The visiting Irish* Taoiseach, Bertie *Ahern, makes the traditional presentation of a bowl of fresh shamrock to the American President. Ahern's meeting with President Clinton on St. Patrick's Day 1998, came as both men were helping to coax through the Good Friday Agreement setting up a new Assembly for Northern Ireland.*

BELOW: *Speaker Tip O'Neill introduced an annual 17 March Speaker's Lunch on Capitol Hill to entertain visiting politicians and the media.*

ABOVE: *All over the world St. Patrick's Day revelers like a drink. Gallagher's Pub could be anywhere: Australia, North America, Britain, even Ireland itself! In fact it is in Pittsburgh, PA.*

every town and city (boosting Guinness sales by 30 percent in 1997 alone.) Secondly, some seven million Australians claim Irish ancestry and are keen to shout about it. And, finally, because March falls right at the end of a baking hot summer, when the daytime heat loses a little of its intensity and it's possible to get drunk during the day without suffering terminal dehydration.

Bar owners, determined to pull in the early custom, will generally compete to offer the lowest-priced Irish breakfast. The idea is that a good fry-up "lines the stomach," allowing greater consumption of alcohol in the hours ahead. With admirable marketing nous, the same bars will advise that eating a "Full Irish" is also the best way to end a drinking session. As a result Irish pub breakfasts tend to attract a bizarre mix of the stone-cold sober and the brain-blastingly drunk, depending on where in the St. Patrick's Day celebration cycle they find themselves. As the Irish themselves say, you wouldn't miss it for quids.

The Dan O'Connell Hotel in Carlton, Melbourne, is a good

example of the logistical horrors facing publicans. Here the park next door is fenced off and becomes an extension of the hotel with its own bar, monster fridge, and toilets. More than a hundred bartenders are recruited for the day and around 8,000 revelers will drink seven weeks worth of trade inside 24 hours. Some even bring along their own sofas and armchairs to make the park feel more like home.

Several other Australian cities are acquiring reputations as the places to be on March 17. These include Darwin, capital of the Northern Territory, which shrugs off the last downpours of its rainy season with a 2,000-strong street party, Brisbane, which boasts a ninety-float grand parade, and Sydney, which hosts the country's biggest march culminating in an open-air music concert. In these cities, fashion sense is tossed out of the

BELOW: *The shady peace of St Stephen's Green, Dublin. On St. Patrick's Day the place is teeming with hundreds of people anxious to begin their march.*

ABOVE: *Mythology on parade in Dublin. Organizers change the theme each year to ensure spectators never get bored.*

window at festival time in favor of green-ness. The ultimate in head-gear, naturally, is a green foam hat with protruding plastic shamrocks.

Inevitably, some celebrations attract controversy. *Amach*, an Irish gay and lesbian support group, has in the past been refused permission to join the Sydney parade while the "Queensland Irish Association" dinner has traditionally been a men-only affair, inviting accusations that it betrays St. Patrick's own open-door philosophy.

In the face of all this, some of the older Australian towns do stick stubbornly to tradition. Westbury, in northern Tasmania, for instance takes great pride in commemorating its most famous rebel—John Mitchel.

The story goes that, in 1848, seven leaders of the "Young Ireland" revolutionary movement were transported to Tasmania (then known as Van Diemen's Land) for their part in rebel activities. Four of them escaped from the island and the authorities demanded that the others gave an undertaking not to follow. Mitchel, the most radical of the new arrivals, agreed but then renounced his pledge at Bothwell and began a daring series of adventures to reach freedom. He borrowed a horse and, in the middle of winter, rode across the wild, central plain of Tasmania to Westbury. Here he was harbored by Irish sympathizers who frustrated searches by the British troops for weeks. After several abortive attempts to reach the coast, he disguised himself as a priest and journeyed to Hobart on a public coach. Among his fellow passengers was the recently-retired Attorney General. Sadly, history does not record their conversation en route.

Mitchel boarded a ship at Hobart and made it back to Ireland. Some of his fellow-rebels sought a new life in North America, carving out successful careers in the process. Among them was Thomas Meagher, a Brigadier-General in the Civil War and later Governor of Montana.

In Europe, outside the Irish Republic, St. Patrick's Day today tends to be a curious mix of "drink-to-old-Ireland" hype (generated by bar owners) and Celtic cultural hype (generated

BELOW: *Some of the fantastic models which adorned Dublin city center on March 17, 1996.*

ABOVE: *A Green Detective scans the Dublin crowd to spot prize-winners. Anyone dressed extravagantly in green stands a chance.*

ABOVE RIGHT: *Decking out houses is another traditionally Irish-American way of celebrating St. Patrick's Feast Day. Some residents just don't know when to stop!*

BELOW RIGHT: *Parading in Chicago. On March 17 there are very few citizens who can't find a hint of Irish blood in their family roots.*

by academics). When the *Irish Times* asked its correspondents around the world to pen a few lines of local color on international festivities there were some intriguing contrasts.

The Frankfurt correspondent, for instance, pleaded that he "could not find any non pub-related event" apart from a march in Munich and a St. Patrick's concert which occurred two days late on March 19. The Paris staff writer, however, reported a plethora of Irish cultural events, including public lectures with titles such as "The Story and the Storyteller in Irish Tradition," "Reinventing Ireland: Culture and Politics" and even "Les Clichés Transfigures Du Theatre Irlandais." It seems there's nothing like reinforcing national stereotypes when you're stuck for a story!

The Belgians don't generally go in for parades, so events in Brussels—the European Community's political hub—inevitably tend to center around pubs and the annual dinner of the "Irish Club." There is also a "Gaelic Club" sports afternoon at which four teams of ex-pats representing the provinces compete in a Gaelic football tournament and hurling match.

RIGHT: *High hats; high fashion. Outfits like these have helped the Dublin parade become a unique social occasion.*

BELOW: *Stepping out for Patrick in Pittsburgh. The city's industry attracted many emigrants during the early twentieth century.*

Ireland's European Commissioner, meanwhile, hosts what is generally regarded as the liveliest event of the Brussels calendar on the eighth floor of the Breydel Commission headquarters. Senior officials from his cabinet gratefully shed their greymen aura to pull pints, tell stories, and sing songs. This is what international diplomacy is all about.

In the UK, the city of Manchester leads the way with a ten-day Irish festival attracting 100,000 visitors. Sponsored by Guinness and the City Council, the stated aim is to "broaden people's minds and explore the wealth of Irish culture." Although organized theater, films, concerts, and live comedy provide the main attractions, there is also a true community feel to the festival with local pubs and clubs setting their own agendas and a traditional Irish craft market.

Perhaps Europe's most novel St. Patrick's Day march is in Moscow, where the locals grew up believing that a parade had to include several megatons of atomic warhead to be worth a candle. These days Russian spectators easily outnumber the foreign community along the Novy Arbat, cheering on an eclectic mix of Cossack horsemen and bare-legged majorettes. Having parades for fun is a relatively new concept to Muscovites (attendance for the May 1, Labor Day march used

ABOVE AND RIGHT: *Images of Dublin's St. Patrick's Festival. Once the poor relation of the worldwide celebration the city now offers a parade full of innovation and originality.*

to be compulsory) but they have taken up the idea with alacrity. The Novy Arbat event has become hugely popular with young children. Doubtless Patrick himself would have approved.

Moscow's other main Irish social is the "Annual Emerald Ball" held in the old Penta Hotel (now the Olympic Renaissance). This is a fund-raiser for city orphanage No. 24, an institution which has been supported by the local Irish community for decades. It is usually followed on the Sunday before the parade by mass at the Church of St. Louis des Français, in the shadow of the former KGB headquarters.

Which leaves us dear old Ireland herself, once the poor relation of St. Patrick's Day partying; now a model for innovation. Given that the Irish have absolutely no tradition of holding parades on March 17; they have cottoned on pretty quickly to how it should be done.

The big event kicks off at St. Stephen's Green in the morning and follows the ubiquitous "theme" notion. In 1998 the "magic" theme included a model dragon, a theater group portraying the ancient rituals of the shamen, an Aladdin's lamp pageant, a Harley-Davidson motorbike convoy, a giant rabbit performing magic tricks, jugglers, acrobats, clowns, trapeze artists and the "Green Detectives" who mingle with spectators handing out spot prizes to anyone who has opted to "Dress Loud; Dress Green."

What St. Patrick would make of it all, God alone knows. Sticklers for traditional culture, and the devoutly religious, will no doubt find the modern global festivals distasteful and an affront to the life-work of a great and brave missionary. Yet compared to the commercialization of Christmas, St. Patrick's Day is positively low-key. If nothing else it at least reminds the Irish of a story in which faith and hope triumphed against all odds.

For an island struggling to find peace, it's a story worth remembering.

LEFT: *Selling Patrick memorabilia and banners at Pittsburgh; March 17, 1996.*

TODAY'S BIGGEST
U.S. ST. PATRICK'S
DAY PARADES

City	Floats	Marchers	Crowd (millions)	Route (miles)	Duration (hours)
Boston	100	10,000	1.1	3.2	3.0
Chicago	200	20,000	0.2	1.0	2.0
New York	75	150,000	2.0–3.0	1.5	5.5
Philadelphia	100	9,700	0.25	2.6	5.0
Savannah	250	10,000	0.5	3.2	3.0–4.0

Today's Biggest U.S. St. Patrick's Day Parades

FAR LEFT: *The dramatic view over Boston harbor and city at sunrise. Boston remains a spiritual home for Irish-Americanism.*

LEFT: *A ticker-tape spectacular in honor of St. Patrick as seen from State Street, Chicago.*

BELOW: *Harry S. Truman offers his support to New York's parade organizers in 1948.*

TOP: *It could hardly be called a traditional costume but this reveler in Chicago doesn't seem too bothered.*

RIGHT: *One of the 200 or so floats which wind their way slowly through Chicago every March 17.*

FAR RIGHT: *Smoking a clay pipe became the hallmark of Irish emigrants—women as well as men. This Chicago marcher proudly continues the tradition.*

U.S. CITIES:
PERCENTAGE OF IRISH
POPULATION TODAY
(BASED ON 1990 CENSUS)

City	Total	Irish	Irish %
Boston	574,283	128,682	22
Philadelphia	1,585,577	268,280	16
Kansas City	435,141	72,064	16
Seattle	516,259	72,718	14
St. Louis	396,685	51,774	13
Dallas	1,006,831	104,581	10
San Francisco	723,959	73,792	10
Savannah	137,557	13,975	10
Chicago	2,783,726	237,312	8
New York	7,322,564	535,846	7
Los Angeles	3,485,398	195,635	5
Detroit	1,027,974	38,268	3

RIGHT: *No occupant of the White House can afford to ignore the Irish vote.*

FAR RIGHT: *Repairs to the Statue of Liberty — another New York landmark which owes much to the efforts of Irish laborers.*

ABOVE: *Emigrants arriving in America in 1923 sit down to a welcome meal. Too often the welcome did not extend to good housing and employment.*

RIGHT: *Chaotic scenes at a U.S. Immigration Office in 1904. America needed Irish emigrants to service its immense industrial economy. But many employers were openly racist. Employment advertisements often carried the hated line: "No Irish Need Apply."*

THE CROAGH PATRICK PILGRIMAGE

ABOVE: *On a day of scattered cloud, sunlight playing across the summit of Croagh Patrick gives the mountain a mystical quality.*

RIGHT: *The craggy slopes of Croagh Patrick rise menacingly above a nearby golf course. Services are held in a small stone church at the top of the mountain on the last Sunday in July.*

FOR THOSE WHO TODAY CELEBRATE St. Patrick's life from a more religious perspective, a pilgrimage to the summit of Croagh Patrick is regarded as spiritually important.

Some climb the stony track in bare feet—a gesture both to honor the saint and to do penance for sins—and until 1974 a few diehards even navigated the path by night (the Irish climate and hostile terrain eventually convinced them that this was not a good idea.) St. Patrick's Day is invariably popular with pilgrims but walkers can be seen on the slopes most days. Around 100,000 a year have now established a well-worn path to the top.

Whichever method you choose, the mountain, at 765m—just over 2,500ft—is a literally breathtaking experience. Croagh Patrick, or "The Reek" as it is known to locals, is arguably Ireland's most famous summit. It is certainly one of the most beautiful, dominating the skyline of Co. Mayo's unspoiled west coast and offering spectacular views. Its fame derives from the

legend that Patrick led his followers here for a forty-day fast in A.D. 441, emulating the acts of Christ and Moses in the Holy Land. It is apparently during this fast that Patrick banished all Irish snakes to a hollow named by chroniclers of the day as *Lug na Demon.*

In fact, St. Patrick was by no means the first to live (albeit temporarily) on "The Reek." There are traces of a well-fortified prehistoric earthworks at the summit, complete with stone ramparts and hut remains. Beads dating from the third century B.C. have been recovered.

The pilgrimage begins at St. Patrick's statue, erected by a priest in 1928, and takes about five hours to complete (three up; two down.) For many visitors, among them the late Princess Grace of Monaco, this stone figure is the furthest they get up the deceptively gentle-looking slope.

In the eighteenth century it was said that an old hermit known as "Bob of the Reek" lived on the summit and "was the boy for doing penance for those who were unable of coming themselves to the Reek." Bob survived on Croagh Patrick for fourteen years and was eventually buried beside the little stone church on the summit. His is the only funeral to have been held there although in times past the church has hosted four weddings. It is now closed for much of the year and the only services are held on the last Sunday of July (known as Reek Sunday).

POTA PHADRAIG
(PATRICK'S POT)

THE ST. PATRICK'S DAY TRADITION of drinking a glass of whiskey containing a floating shamrock was supposedly started by the saint himself. The legend goes that Patrick was given a short measure of whiskey by an innkeeper and took revenge by unleashing a fire-and-brimstone speech on the hapless man. Patrick warned that the devil lay in the publican's cellar feasting on his cheating nature.

Next time he was passing, Patrick called in for another

medicinal tipple and found the landlord filling everyone's glasses to overflowing. He and his host stepped down into the cellar where they saw the devil "starving from generosity." Patrick banished the evil one from the property and decreed that thereafter everyone should drink a tot of whiskey on his feast day. This became known as "Patrick's Pot," although the "drowning of the Shamrock" seems to have been a much later adaptation of the ritual.

ABOVE: *Dun Duchathair (The Black Fort) on Inishmore. Ancient sites such as this are steeped in legend; sometimes intertwining pagan doctrine with Patrick's brand of Christianity.*

GLOBAL SHAMROCK

ABOVE: *Most graffiti in Northern Ireland preaches the language of war. Here a shamrock motif puts the case for peace.*

IRISH UNIFORMED PERSONNEL are often presented with a shamrock to wear on St. Patrick's Day. To ensure diplomats abroad can share this tradition, Ireland's national airline, Aer Lingus, which has a distinctive green shamrock emblem on the tails of its planes, flies fresh supplies of the plant to Irish embassies everywhere.

PREVIOUS PAGE: *The Queen Mother pictured in 1997 at her annual St. Patrick's Day presentation of shamrock to the First Battalion Irish Guards. The regiment's mascot, Cuchlain the Irish wolfhound, also "wears the green."*

RIGHT: *Pope John Paul II waves to wellwishers as he prepares to leave Ireland. The shamrock motif which adorns Aer Lingus planes (see also above) is instantly recognizable—helping to promote Irish culture around the world.*

CATHEDRALS DEDICATED TO ST. PATRICK

BELOW: *Intricately carved stonework in the chancel of St. Patrick's Church of Ireland Cathedral, Armagh, is testament to the skill of Victorian craftsmen.*

RIGHT: *The superb façade of St. Patrick's Cathedral, New York.*

Wherever you find Irish communities around the world, the chances are that a church or cathedral dedicated to their patron saint won't be far away. St. Patrick's Church of Ireland Cathedral and St. Patrick's Roman Catholic Cathedral, both close to Patrick's original "see" at Armagh, are the best known, though St. Patrick's in Dublin is equally magnificent. Elsewhere, New York City and Fort Worth, Texas, each boast beautiful cathedrals dedicated to the saint, as does Melbourne, Australia. St. Patrick's Cathedral, Barbados, stands out among the more exotic locations.

RIGHT: *The classic lines of St. Patrick's Cathedral, New York, contrast sharply with the modern architecture nearby. The cathedral seats 2,200 people and its* Pietà *is three times larger than the* Pietà *at St. Peter's, Rome.*

ST. PATRICK'S
CHURCH OF IRELAND CATHEDRAL
ARMAGH

RIGHT: *A gleaming brass eagle forms the lecturn inside St. Patrick's Church of Ireland Cathedral at Armagh.*

FAR RIGHT: *An interior view of the cathedral, which dates from the mid-thirteenth century. It has been attacked on at least seventeen occasions but painstaking restoration work has ensured its glory remains.*

THE OLDER OF ARMAGH'S TWO CATHEDRALS, this building is based on a design produced by Archbishop O'Scanlain in 1268. It has been attacked on at least seventeen separate occasions but always repaired. The last large-scale restoration occurred between 1834 and 1840 under the auspices of Archbishop Lord George Beresford.

Among its collection of artifacts is a Celtic cross dating from the eleventh century, a fifteenth-century stone altar, and an octagonal-shaped Baptismal font.

ST. PATRICK'S
ROMAN CATHOLIC CATHEDRAL ARMAGH

BELOW RIGHT: *The sense of space inside the Roman Catholic St. Patrick's Cathedral rarely fails to inspire visitors. The interior is based on an Italianate Victorian Gothic style.*

FAR RIGHT: *St. Patrick's Roman Catholic cathedral at Armagh is sited close to the saint's original "see." The foundation stone was laid in 1840.*

THIS WAS DEDICATED ON AUGUST 24, 1873, at a cost of about Ir£70,000. It was the dream of Archbishop William Crolly, who laid the foundation stone in 1840. When he died during the famine, building work ground to a halt and was not restarted until 1854. A new Bishop, Dr. Dixon, resolved to have construction work finished and employed architects to develop a more Gothic appearance. However, it was not until Bishop McGettigan was installed in 1870 that the finishing exterior touches were applied. The interior was completed early this century.

ST. PATRICK'S CATHEDRAL, DUBLIN

SET ON THE OLDEST Christian site in Dublin, St. Patrick is supposed to have baptized converts here using water from a nearby well. The original fifth-century building was adapted by the Normans in 1191 and the present structure dates from the thirteenth century. Ireland's first university was founded at the cathedral in 1320.

The west tower, 37m high (121ft) with walls 3m (nearly 10ft) thick, is topped by a 31m (102ft) spire and houses the largest peal of bells in Ireland. One of Dublin's first public clocks was placed on the cathedral walls in 1560.

The vault contains the remains of the writer Jonathan Swift, author of *Gulliver's Travels*.

ABOVE: *An illustration from Swift's classic allegorical novel* Gulliver's Travels *captioned "Gulliver visited by a Lilliputian Noble." The author was a vituperative social and political satirist.*

LEFT: *One of Ireland's greatest writers, Jonathan Swift (1667–1745), was a former Dean of St. Patrick's, Dublin. His remains are held in the vault. This portrait was painted around 1720.*

ST. PATRICK'S CATHEDRAL, NEW YORK

BELOW: *Gothic island in a sea of skyscrapers. An aerial view of St. Patrick's Cathedral, New York, taken in 1961.*

RIGHT: *A dramatic photograph of the cathedral at night, with the Atlas statue illuminated in the foreground.*

BUILDING WORK BEGAN IN 1858 under the direction of Archbishop John Hughes. The cathedral was opened in May 1879 and the west front towers were added in 1888. Since then, there has been regular restoration and redecoration.

The cathedral, which seats 2,200, has many grand and interesting features including the *Pietà* (three times larger than the *Pietà* in St. Peter's, Rome) and the solid bronze *baldachin* above the main altar. The Archbishops of New York are buried in a crypt beneath the high altar. Their traditional hats, known as *galeros*, hang from a ceiling above the tomb.

RIGHT: *A view of the superb vaulting inside St. Patrick's, New York. Construction began in 1858 but was severly delayed as the builders tried in vain to dig deep enough to hit bedrock. The problem was eventually resolved when a wealthy benefactor donated more money.*

ST. PATRICK'S CATHEDRAL, FORT WORTH

A WOODEN CHURCH WAS BUILT ON THIS SITE IN 1876 but as more catholics settled in Texas, so demand grew for a grander, stone structure. This was commissioned in 1889, on a budget of $110,000, and emerged as one of America's most impressive Gothic buildings. Sadly, a few wooden pews are all that remains of the original church.

ST. PATRICK'S CATHEDRAL, MELBOURNE

RIGHT: *The distinctive skyline of Melbourne, Australia. In one city hotel alone St. Patrick's Day revelers drink the equivalent of seven weeks' trade in 24 hours. More than 100 bartenders have to be specially recruited to cope with the rush.*

T HIS WAS CONSECRATED ON OCTOBER 27, 1897, after almost half-a-century of building work costing a hefty Ir£200,000. Spires were added in 1937 and 1939, and in 1970 the sanctuary was extended. Pope Paul VI declared the cathedral a Minor Basilica in 1974.

ST. PATRICK'S CATHEDRAL, BARBADOS

NEXT PAGE: *Bagpipers of the New York City Police Department's Emerald Society march past St. Patrick's Cathedral on New York's Fifth Avenue during the 1995 St. Patrick's Day Parade.*

T HE ORIGINAL CATHEDRAL, IN BAY STREET, ST. MICHAEL, was built in 1848 but destroyed by fire in 1897—the result of a suspected arson attack by the ruling class of (mainly protestant) planters. Even an island paradise, it seems, failed to defuse religious bigotry. The cathedral we see today was completed in 1899 and consecrated on August 23, 1903.